So Much Tending Remains

So Much Tending Remains

Poems by

Emily Patterson

Cover design by Shay Culligan
Cover image by Annie Spratt

ISBN: 978-1-63980-175-6

Kelsay Books
502 South 1040 East, A-119
American Fork, Utah 84003
Kelsaybooks.com

for Saoirse

Acknowledgments

Gratitude is given to the publications below, where many of these poems first appeared, sometimes in earlier forms:

Anti-Heroin Chic: "Anna Maria Island," "When My Daughter Considers the Magnolia"

Gingernut Magazine: "Birth Plans"

Mom Egg Review: "Near the Fourth of July in a Pandemic"

Mothers Always Write: "Two Moccasins Tied Together," "When You Were Nine Weeks Old"

The Mum Poem Press: "The First Time You Crawled," "Sunflowers," "Tale of Two Squirrels"

Raine Poetry Publishing: "Night Walk"

Rearing in the Rearview, Quillkeepers Press: "To My Daughter Eating Toast"

Songs of Love and Strength: An Anthology of Poems on Motherhood, edited by Katharine Perry: "Hunger"

Sparks of Calliope: "Fruits from My Hand"

The Sunlight Press: "The Nights Were a Wilderness"

Thimble Literary Magazine: "At Elyse's Baby Shower"

—

"The Nights Were a Wilderness" and "When My Daughter Considers the Magnolia" were also anthologized in *Sapling* by Quillkeepers Press.

Contents

Near the Fourth of July in a Pandemic 11

Birth Plans 12

Hunger 13

Someday I'll Tell You about the Social Worker 14

Two Moccasins Tied Together 15

Sunflowers 16

A Day Comes When Your Lungs Are Full
of Weather 17

Tale of Two Squirrels 18

When You Were Nine Weeks Old 19

At Elyse's Baby Shower 20

In Praise of Hands 21

Drop-off 22

Night Walk 23

Counterpoint 24

To My Daughter Eating Toast 25

The Nights Were a Wilderness 26

Mother of Mine 27

When My Daughter Considers the Magnolia 28

The First Time You Crawled, 29

Anna Maria Island 30

Fruits from My Hand 31

So Much Tending Remains 32

Near the Fourth of July in a Pandemic

The summer you were born, fireworks sputtered and crackled every night for weeks, briefly luminous. Roused from sleep by the weight of you, I heard them still, even as the sky blued. One hand to my belly to catch your kicks, I wondered who stayed awake lighting fuse after fuse—igniting Chrysanthemums and Catherine Wheels, ashes settling in the grass like spent confetti, beads of light growing dim against the dawn. When I finally held your body to mine, near that Fourth of July in a pandemic, I wondered how to tell you about this, the summer you were born: These months marked equally by fever and fear, a closeness heavy in the lungs, air sulfured—as well as all the joy I could bear in your brand-new eyes, two lights radiating everywhere, turning the weary world into the brightest place I'd ever dreamed.

Birth Plans

That summer, I spent hours
searching for the perfect gown.
Soft blue cotton, buttons at the front.

We left our luggage in the car,
visions of time in our minds—
hours walking the bright halls.

Instead: tangled smock
around my body like a torn vine.
Four centimeters, then nine.

Hurried midwife, room alight,
then you—born with the dawn.

My blue gown tucked away
neatly, your eyes the color
of night.

Hunger

That first time, your body
across mine under bulbs brighter

than day, you chirped
and bobbed your downy head

as my hands learned to hold you,
as the nurse pressed my flesh

so you could breathe and eat,
a primal determination

in your twiggy fingers, tiny *O*
of a mouth catching golden beads

in wild gulps—your hunger,
insistent as my own,

unfolding into this world
like wings.

Someday I'll Tell You about the Social Worker

In a room with white walls, white floor
speckled like an egg, and white sheets:

You are hours old and wrapped in a white
blanket, waking every hour to eat.

A kind social worker visits
our room, tells me the signs

of *more than baby blues.*
I nod, but my eyes stray

to you. I am all jubilance,
distracted by sleepless joy.

Later, as the days and nights
blur, I'll remember her words.

They will be reassuringly warm
as the first sip of tea. They will taste

of a courage both bitter and honeyed.

Two Moccasins Tied Together

Lakeside Chautauqua, Ohio

The first time I heard your cry
outside, I was struck by its
smallness: how it hardly

seemed to reach the twin
Catalpas in our front yard,
shedding their green pods;

how it landed so softly
on the world. Inside the house,
it filled our small rooms, filled

my whole body with your sound;
like when I breathed in your smell,
and it was morning sun and wheat

fields, everywhere. That summer
at the lake we watched the rough
grey waters, thick haze, clustered

gulls. It was what I craved,
I'll admit: to feel small beside
you, to be held by the world

just as I held you.

Sunflowers

Those days were for moving thin rivers
of milk from my body to yours. Leaves,
newly golden, skidded over the pavement
like husks, lovely but worn. I poured my
morning coffee over ice in the afternoons.
Acorns clogged the curb. I often forgot
to eat, tried not to count the purple streaks
on my breasts and my back. Clothes
went unfolded. An enthusiastic cricket
got trapped somewhere in the basement.
My mind hazy as a lullaby, as if the days
were, in some ways, already memories.
In the garden off the alley we found
a patch of sunflowers by accident.
They were covered in small bees.
I tugged the thick gold petals,
then let them go. It was enough.

A Day Comes When Your Lungs Are Full
of Weather

and all night you cough,
cling to me in the dark.

All night I ease
us back to sleep

briefly. Each time
you wake, I nearly

stagger, head on fire,
yet my body goes on

to make milk,
goes on to sweep

damp hair from
your cheek, goes on.

When morning
graces our bodies

and swallows sing
outside your window,

I close my eyes,
settle into the sound,

remember there are
so many ways

to be mothered
by this world.

Tale of Two Squirrels

The leaves on the Catalpa have gone gold with age, and the sky is an enamel bowl, practically cerulean. I see it through the bathroom window, where I sometimes come to hide while you are crying; where I sometimes stand while you are sleeping and I cannot, bare feet on the cold tile, exhaustion on my heels; where I once watched a young squirrel grasp a thin branch in terror, his mother below, too heavy to follow. Eventually he dropped, paws stretched to tiny brown stars, landing on the grass unharmed. With her teeth, she lugged him back to their nest in a series of Herculean leaps. I was too tired to make any kind of lesson out of this, only knew that I felt like both squirrels, somehow: waiting, tending, letting go, carrying and being carried, all at once.

When You Were Nine Weeks Old

Early autumn, we emerge
from our shared sleep haze,

drive Ohio backroads
to the orchard for Galas,

delicata, dough doused
in sugar so thick it sticks

to our teeth. We pick apples,
palm-sized and sun-warmed,

wandering the rows until
all we see is September sky,

a choir of trees, and each
other: a specific universe,

both familiar and new,
briefly ours alone.

At Elyse's Baby Shower

You wake up hungry and hollering so we leave the other
guests, wandering the church basement hallway to find
an empty meeting room where I sit on a folding chair
to feed you as sunlight dyes the room gold. The carpet
is undeniably seventies, yarn-like, a potpourri palette,
and there's the smell of old books, although the shelves
are bare. I notice your hair growing lighter, catching
the sun like water, and your eyes, too, have recently
gone from navy to lake blue. It is our first October
together. Last year I was five weeks pregnant and
afraid. Now I hear Elyse in the other room, saying
thank you again and again, crumpling tissue, tearing
paper, unveiling the artifacts of new life. Now I rest
in golden light, feeding my own child, saying silently,
again and again: *Thank you thank you thank you.*

In Praise of Hands

That year we picked Sun Golds
and Black Pearls into October.

You were discovering your hands,
forming fists you tried to eat like plums.

I rinsed the tomatoes in the sink
and they became wet jewels.

All afternoon, my hands held you
as you slept, held the scent

of green vines for hours.
Your small fingers, shiny

with spit, clasped in clumsy prayer:
the holiest things I'd seen.

Drop-off

I leave you
and your tiny bundle

with another loving woman
who is not your mother.

Some days are like this,
my body grieving

the lack of you,
weighted as if

I carry you
within me again.

Night Walk

After ten minutes, you cry out.
My whole body braces
for the awakening.

Sometimes you settle back
into sleep, and my relief
is cosmic, comical.

But at seven months, you've learned
to resist slumber—too immersed
in this world now to tumble
in and out of naps.

Some nights, we walk instead:
you in your rose-pink snowsuit,
me in my wool socks and hat.

Up, down the darkening streets,
listening to air move between
cars on the nearby freeway.

Your lashes rest on your cheeks,
or not. The cars hum, not unlike
an ocean.

Counterpoint

You are playing a five-note piano
with rainbow keys, the G a little sharp.

You can sit on your own now, but lately
you don't sleep while the sun is out.

I have the record player and vacuum
going; I'm buzzing through rooms

while you're still content, trying not
to replay the phrase in my mind

that I might be losing my mind;
that I might be losing something

else, though I'm not sure what.
The windchill is twelve today,

the white winter light so electric,
I almost hear it: briefly in harmony

with both your song and mine.

To My Daughter Eating Toast

Your hand hovers beyond the tray
as you contemplate whether to let go.
Eventually, you decide:

Yes, you will unfurl your fist
to send the bread, crushed and soggy,
to the floor.

Yes, you will fold over the chair's edge
to find the dog below, grateful for your gift.

Yes, you will smile at me, revealing
the scraps of toast that made it, somehow,
into your small pink grin of a mouth.

Yes—may you always look to me
this way, expecting to be found
marvelous.

The Nights Were a Wilderness

Spring, waking at last. Birdsong
audible through the walls. The sun
taking back the six o'clock hour.

One night you slept in your room,
waking only once. I felt reborn.
The next, you nursed three times

an hour. I knew enough not to be
surprised. Still, after you drifted
into dreams, I held on,

felt you surrender to slumber
then cradled you longer. Soon
it would be morning, maybe

it already was. I knew enough
not to mind the time. To let the day
make its way to us, a tentative animal,

like the deer in the nearby ravine,
all bold eyes and stillness,
bodies not quite tame.

Mother of Mine

Her short hair shimmers across her forehead,
pearl-white as the scoop of an oyster shell.

She cares for you on Mondays and Tuesdays,
sipping black coffee that always, always,

goes cold in its cup. Upstairs, I stare
into the screen, listen to the two of you:

joy made audible in shrieks and praises,
books read in rhyming lines, the chair's

gentle creaks. You sleep. When you wake,
you might wonder after me, mostly as a body

that feeds you. I don't mind. This mother
of mine lavishes love on you in waves:

clear, cool water cascading over you,
over me—channels both familiar and new.

When My Daughter Considers the Magnolia

I wasn't ready to tell you about
loss, but the magnolia tree

in the alley bloomed early,
then died in a late frost.

Its once plush petals
silent as dead leaves.

I wasn't ready to explain
how these things can seem

personal, how they hold
the prick of betrayal.

But you don't call them
beautiful or otherwise.

Each morning you awaken
to the world, all of it

worthy of your wonder.

The First Time You Crawled,

a kind woman who was not me
placed a tiny plastic turtle

just out of reach and you did it—
inched your left knee forward,

then the right, lifted each palm,
planted it again. Movement, born.

I saw all of this in a video I watched
repeatedly, pretending each time

that it was happening just then,
that I was there to praise you, too.

There are at least two mothers
in me—one who celebrates

as you keep moving
through this world, the other

quietly pressing *play* once more.

Anna Maria Island

When you still spoke your own language,
we took you to meet the ocean.

The view was one swirl of cool blue,
waves and sky telling the same story.

You pushed your toes through creamy sand,
conversed with yourself while I listened.

Were you telling the world all you knew?
Were you remembering what it no longer could?

Maybe I knew these sounds, once:
your water music, a language I lost as I grew.

I picked up my book again.
Your story was for you.

Fruits from My Hand

On the wood floor you play
with a set of wooden fruits:

wedge of watermelon, pear
perfectly sized to your palm,

and your favorite, the bright
lemon that rolls in a spiral.

You screech as it curls
just beyond your reach,

and I delight in how simply
I can offer what you seek.

Taking the fruits from my hand,
you fling them to the floor again

and again—purposefully,
not looking at me, until

I begin to see: It's you
who will choose

how to move through
this world, into yourself.

So Much Tending Remains

You settle on a single ribbon
of grass, so green it glows.

Studying its clean curve intently,
you begin to sing to yourself.

Already, you possess
a growing gift for aloneness,

content to consider a soft
sleeve, the shape of your own

plump palm—to inhabit
the universe of you.

So much tending remains,
yet I see the space between us

grow, a tiny green thing
that spirals toward the light.

About the Author

Emily Patterson received her B.A. in English from Ohio Wesleyan University, where she was awarded the F.L. Hunt Prize and Marie Drennan Prize for Poetry, and her M.A. in Education from The Ohio State University. Her work has been nominated for a Pushcart Prize and appears in *Minerva Rising Press, The Sunlight Press, Sheila-Na-Gig, Literary Mama, The Mum Poem Press, Oyster River Pages, Sky Island Journal,* and elsewhere. She lives with her family in Columbus, Ohio.

www.ingramcontent.com/pod-product-compliance
Lightning Source LLC
Chambersburg PA
CBHW030816090426
42737CB00010B/1296